Where Does the
MONEY GO?
Monthly Budget/Planner

@ Journals and Notebooks

@ Journals & Notebooks

All Rights reserved. No part of this book may be reproduced or used in any way or form or by any means whether electronic or mechanical, this means that you cannot record or photocopy any material ideas or tips that are provided in this book.

Copyright 2016

Monthly Planner and Expense Tracker

Month of _____

Expenses	Budget	Actual
Subtotals		

Income
_____

Other Income
_____

Total Income
_____

Total Actual Expenses
_____

Remaining Balance
_____

Notes

Credits	Savings	Goals

Monthly Planner and Expense Tracker

Month of _____

Expenses	Budget	Actual
Subtotals		

Income
_____

Other Income
_____

Total Income
_____

Total Actual Expenses
_____

Remaining Balance
_____

Notes

Credits	Savings	Goals

Monthly Planner and Expense Tracker

Month of _____

Expenses	Budget	Actual
Subtotals		

Income
_____

Other Income
_____

Total Income
_____

Total Actual Expenses
_____

Remaining Balance
_____

Notes

Credits	Savings	Goals

Monthly Planner and Expense Tracker

Month of _____

Expenses	Budget	Actual
Subtotals		

Income _____

Other Income _____

Total Income _____

Total Actual Expenses _____

Remaining Balance _____

Notes

Credits

Savings

Goals

Monthly Planner and Expense Tracker

Month of _____

Expenses	Budget	Actual
Subtotals		

Income

Other Income

Total Income

Total Actual Expenses

Remaining Balance

Notes

Credits

Savings

Goals

Monthly Planner and Expense Tracker

Month of _____

Expenses	Budget	Actual
Subtotals		

Income
_____

Other Income
_____

Total Income
_____

Total Actual Expenses
_____

Remaining Balance
_____

Notes

Credits	Savings	Goals

Monthly Planner and Expense Tracker

Month of _____

Expenses	Budget	Actual
Subtotals		

Income

Other Income

Total Income

Total Actual Expenses

Remaining Balance

Notes

Credits	Savings	Goals

Monthly Planner and Expense Tracker

Month of _____

Expenses	Budget	Actual
Subtotals		

Income
_____

Other Income
_____

Total Income
_____

Total Actual Expenses
_____

Remaining Balance
_____

Notes

Credits	Savings	Goals

Monthly Planner and Expense Tracker

Month of _____

Expenses	Budget	Actual
Subtotals		

Income

Other Income

Total Income

Total Actual Expenses

Remaining Balance

Notes

Credits	Savings	Goals

Monthly Planner and Expense Tracker

Month of _____

Expenses	Budget	Actual
Subtotals		

Income
_____

Other Income
_____

Total Income
_____

Total Actual Expenses
_____

Remaining Balance
_____

Notes

Credits	Savings	Goals

Monthly Planner and Expense Tracker

Month of _____

Expenses	Budget	Actual
Subtotals		

Income
_____

Other Income
_____

Total Income
_____

Total Actual Expenses
_____

Remaining Balance
_____

Notes

Credits	Savings	Goals

Monthly Planner and Expense Tracker

Month of _____

Expenses	Budget	Actual
Subtotals		

Income

Other Income

Total Income

Total Actual Expenses

Remaining Balance

Notes

Credits

Savings

Goals

Monthly Planner and Expense Tracker

Month of _____

Expenses	Budget	Actual
Subtotals		

Income _____

Other Income _____

Total Income _____

Total Actual Expenses _____

Remaining Balance _____

Notes

Credits	Savings	Goals

Monthly Planner and Expense Tracker

Month of _____

Expenses	Budget	Actual
Subtotals		

Income
_____

Other Income
_____

Total Income
_____

Total Actual Expenses
_____

Remaining Balance
_____

Notes

Credits	Savings	Goals

Monthly Planner and Expense Tracker

Month of _____

Expenses	Budget	Actual
Subtotals		

Income

Other Income

Total Income

Total Actual Expenses

Remaining Balance

Notes

Credits

Savings

Goals

Monthly Planner and Expense Tracker

Month of _____

Expenses	Budget	Actual
Subtotals		

Income
_____

Other Income
_____

Total Income
_____

Total Actual Expenses
_____

Remaining Balance
_____

Notes

Credits	Savings	Goals

Monthly Planner and Expense Tracker

Month of _____

Expenses	Budget	Actual
Subtotals		

Income
_____

Other Income
_____

Total Income
_____

Total Actual Expenses
_____

Remaining Balance
_____

Notes

Credits

Savings

Goals

Monthly Planner and Expense Tracker

Month of _____

Expenses	Budget	Actual
Subtotals		

Income
_____

Other Income
_____

Total Income
_____

Total Actual Expenses
_____

Remaining Balance
_____

Notes

Credits	Savings	Goals

Expenses	Budget	Actual
Subtotals		

Monthly Planner and Expense Tracker

Month of _____

Income
_____

Other Income
_____

Total Income
_____

Total Actual Expenses
_____

Remaining Balance
_____

Notes

Credits	Savings	Goals

Monthly Planner and Expense Tracker

Month of _____

Expenses	Budget	Actual
Subtotals		

Income
_____

Other Income
_____

Total Income
_____

Total Actual Expenses
_____

Remaining Balance
_____

Notes

Credits	Savings	Goals

Monthly Planner and Expense Tracker

Month of _____

Expenses	Budget	Actual
Subtotals		

Income _____

Other Income _____

Total Income _____

Total Actual Expenses _____

Remaining Balance _____

Notes _____

Credits	Savings	Goals

Monthly Planner and Expense Tracker

Month of _____

Expenses	Budget	Actual
Subtotals		

Income

Other Income

Total Income

Total Actual Expenses

Remaining Balance

Notes

Credits

Savings

Goals

Monthly Planner and Expense Tracker

Month of _____

Expenses	Budget	Actual
Subtotals		

Income _____

Other Income _____

Total Income _____

Total Actual Expenses _____

Remaining Balance _____

Notes

Credits	Savings	Goals

Monthly Planner and Expense Tracker

Month of _____

Expenses	Budget	Actual
Subtotals		

Income
_____

Other Income
_____

Total Income
_____

Total Actual Expenses
_____

Remaining Balance
_____

Notes

Credits	Savings	Goals

Monthly Planner and Expense Tracker

Month of _____

Expenses	Budget	Actual
Subtotals		

Income _____

Other Income _____

Total Income _____

Total Actual Expenses _____

Remaining Balance _____

Notes

Credits

Savings

Goals

Monthly Planner and Expense Tracker

Month of _____

Expenses	Budget	Actual
Subtotals		

Income
_____

Other Income
_____

Total Income
_____

Total Actual Expenses
_____

Remaining Balance
_____

Notes

Credits	Savings	Goals

Monthly Planner and Expense Tracker

Month of _____

Expenses	Budget	Actual
Subtotals		

Income
_____

Other Income
_____

Total Income
_____

Total Actual Expenses
_____

Remaining Balance
_____

Notes

Credits	Savings	Goals

Monthly Planner and Expense Tracker

Month of _____

Expenses	Budget	Actual
Subtotals		

Income

_____

Other Income

_____

Total Income

_____

Total Actual Expenses

_____

Remaining Balance

_____

Notes

Credits

Savings

Goals

Monthly Planner and Expense Tracker

Month of _____

Expenses	Budget	Actual
Subtotals		

Income

Other Income

Total Income

Total Actual Expenses

Remaining Balance

Notes

Credits	Savings	Goals

Monthly Planner and Expense Tracker

Month of _____

Expenses	Budget	Actual
Subtotals		

Income

Other Income

Total Income

Total Actual Expenses

Remaining Balance

Notes

Credits	Savings	Goals

Monthly Planner and Expense Tracker

Month of _____

Expenses	Budget	Actual
Subtotals		

Income _____

Other Income _____

Total Income _____

Total Actual Expenses _____

Remaining Balance _____

Notes

Credits	Savings	Goals

Monthly Planner and Expense Tracker

Month of _____

Expenses	Budget	Actual
Subtotals		

Income

Other Income

Total Income

Total Actual Expenses

Remaining Balance

Notes

Credits

Savings

Goals

Monthly Planner and Expense Tracker

Month of _____

Expenses	Budget	Actual
Subtotals		

Income _____

Other Income _____

Total Income _____

Total Actual Expenses _____

Remaining Balance _____

Notes

Credits	Savings	Goals

Monthly Planner and Expense Tracker

Month of _____

Expenses	Budget	Actual
Subtotals		

Income
_____

Other Income
_____

Total Income
_____

Total Actual Expenses
_____

Remaining Balance
_____

Notes

Credits	Savings	Goals

Monthly Planner and Expense Tracker

Month of _____

Expenses	Budget	Actual
Subtotals		

Income _____

Other Income _____

Total Income _____

Total Actual Expenses _____

Remaining Balance _____

Notes

Credits

Savings

Goals

Monthly Planner and Expense Tracker

Month of _____

Expenses	Budget	Actual
Subtotals		

Income
_____

Other Income
_____

Total Income
_____

Total Actual Expenses
_____

Remaining Balance
_____

Notes

Credits

Savings

Goals

Monthly Planner and Expense Tracker

Month of _____

Expenses	Budget	Actual
Subtotals		

Income

Other Income

Total Income

Total Actual Expenses

Remaining Balance

Notes

Credits	Savings	Goals

Monthly Planner and Expense Tracker

Month of _____

Expenses	Budget	Actual
Subtotals		

Income
_____

Other Income
_____

Total Income
_____

Total Actual Expenses
_____

Remaining Balance
_____

Notes

Credits	Savings	Goals

Monthly Planner and Expense Tracker

Month of _____

Expenses	Budget	Actual
Subtotals		

Income _____

Other Income _____

Total Income _____

Total Actual Expenses _____

Remaining Balance _____

Notes _____

Credits	Savings	Goals

Monthly Planner and Expense Tracker

Month of _____

Expenses	Budget	Actual
Subtotals		

Income
_____

Other Income
_____

Total Income
_____

Total Actual Expenses
_____

Remaining Balance
_____

Notes

Credits	Savings	Goals

Monthly Planner and Expense Tracker

Month of _____

Expenses	Budget	Actual
Subtotals		

Income

Other Income

Total Income

Total Actual Expenses

Remaining Balance

Notes

Credits	Savings	Goals

Monthly Planner and Expense Tracker

Month of _____

Expenses	Budget	Actual
Subtotals		

Income

Other Income

Total Income

Total Actual Expenses

Remaining Balance

Notes

Credits	Savings	Goals

Monthly Planner and Expense Tracker

Month of _____

Expenses	Budget	Actual
Subtotals		

Income _____

Other Income _____

Total Income _____

Total Actual Expenses _____

Remaining Balance _____

Notes

Credits	Savings	Goals

Monthly Planner and Expense Tracker

Month of _____

Expenses	Budget	Actual
Subtotals		

Income
_____

Other Income
_____

Total Income
_____

Total Actual Expenses
_____

Remaining Balance
_____

Notes

Credits

Savings

Goals

Monthly Planner and Expense Tracker

Month of _____

Expenses	Budget	Actual
Subtotals		

Income

Other Income

Total Income

Total Actual Expenses

Remaining Balance

Notes

Credits	Savings	Goals

Monthly Planner and Expense Tracker

Month of _____

Expenses	Budget	Actual
Subtotals		

Income
_____

Other Income
_____

Total Income
_____

Total Actual Expenses
_____

Remaining Balance
_____

Notes

Credits

Savings

Goals

Monthly Planner and Expense Tracker

Month of _____

Expenses	Budget	Actual
Subtotals		

Income

_____

Other Income

_____

Total Income

_____

Total Actual Expenses

_____

Remaining Balance

_____

Notes

Credits	Savings	Goals

Monthly Planner and Expense Tracker

Month of _____

Expenses	Budget	Actual
Subtotals		

Income
_____

Other Income
_____

Total Income
_____

Total Actual Expenses
_____

Remaining Balance
_____

Notes

Credits	Savings	Goals

Monthly Planner and Expense Tracker

Month of _____

Expenses	Budget	Actual
Subtotals		

Income
_____

Other Income
_____

Total Income
_____

Total Actual Expenses
_____

Remaining Balance
_____

Notes

Credits	Savings	Goals

Monthly Planner and Expense Tracker

Month of _____

Expenses	Budget	Actual
Subtotals		

Income
_____

Other Income
_____

Total Income
_____

Total Actual Expenses
_____

Remaining Balance
_____

Notes

Credits	Savings	Goals

Monthly Planner and Expense Tracker

Month of _____

Expenses	Budget	Actual
Subtotals		

Income _____

Other Income _____

Total Income _____

Total Actual Expenses _____

Remaining Balance _____

Notes

Credits	Savings	Goals

Monthly Planner and Expense Tracker

Month of _____

Expenses	Budget	Actual
Subtotals		

Income _____

Other Income _____

Total Income _____

Total Actual Expenses _____

Remaining Balance _____

Notes

Credits	Savings	Goals

Monthly Planner and Expense Tracker

Month of _____

Expenses	Budget	Actual
Subtotals		

Income
_____

Other Income
_____

Total Income
_____

Total Actual Expenses
_____

Remaining Balance
_____

Notes

Credits	Savings	Goals

Monthly Planner and Expense Tracker

Month of _____

Expenses	Budget	Actual
Subtotals		

Income
_____

Other Income
_____

Total Income
_____

Total Actual Expenses
_____

Remaining Balance
_____

Notes

Credits	Savings	Goals

Monthly Planner and Expense Tracker

Month of _____

Expenses	Budget	Actual
Subtotals		

Income
_____
Other Income
_____
Total Income
_____
Total Actual Expenses
_____
Remaining Balance
_____
Notes

Credits	Savings	Goals

Monthly Planner and Expense Tracker

Month of _____

Expenses	Budget	Actual
Subtotals		

Income

Other Income

Total Income

Total Actual Expenses

Remaining Balance

Notes

Credits	Savings	Goals

Monthly Planner and Expense Tracker

Month of _____

Expenses	Budget	Actual
Subtotals		

Income _____

Other Income _____

Total Income _____

Total Actual Expenses _____

Remaining Balance _____

Notes

Credits	Savings	Goals

Monthly Planner and Expense Tracker

Month of _____

Expenses	Budget	Actual
Subtotals		

Income _____

Other Income _____

Total Income _____

Total Actual Expenses _____

Remaining Balance _____

Notes

Credits	Savings	Goals

Monthly Planner and Expense Tracker

Month of _____

Expenses	Budget	Actual
Subtotals		

Income

Other Income

Total Income

Total Actual Expenses

Remaining Balance

Notes

Credits	Savings	Goals

Monthly Planner and Expense Tracker

Month of _____

Expenses	Budget	Actual
Subtotals		

Income
_____
Other Income
_____
Total Income
_____
Total Actual Expenses
_____
Remaining Balance
_____
Notes

Credits	Savings	Goals

Monthly Planner and Expense Tracker

Month of _____

Expenses	Budget	Actual
Subtotals		

Income
_____
Other Income
_____
Total Income
_____
Total Actual Expenses
_____
Remaining Balance
_____
Notes

Credits

Savings

Goals

Monthly Planner and Expense Tracker

Month of _____

Expenses	Budget	Actual
Subtotals		

Income
_____

Other Income
_____

Total Income
_____

Total Actual Expenses
_____

Remaining Balance
_____

Notes

Credits

Savings

Goals

Monthly Planner and Expense Tracker

Month of _____

Expenses	Budget	Actual
Subtotals		

Income

Other Income

Total Income

Total Actual Expenses

Remaining Balance

Notes

Credits	Savings	Goals

Monthly Planner and Expense Tracker

Month of _____

Expenses	Budget	Actual
Subtotals		

Income
_____

Other Income
_____

Total Income
_____

Total Actual Expenses
_____

Remaining Balance
_____

Notes

Credits

Savings

Goals

Monthly Planner and Expense Tracker

Month of _____

Expenses	Budget	Actual
Subtotals		

Income _____

Other Income _____

Total Income _____

Total Actual Expenses _____

Remaining Balance _____

Notes _____

Credits	Savings	Goals

Monthly Planner and Expense Tracker

Month of _____

Expenses	Budget	Actual
Subtotals		

Income

_____

Other Income

_____

Total Income

_____

Total Actual Expenses

_____

Remaining Balance

_____

Notes

Credits	Savings	Goals

Monthly Planner and Expense Tracker

Month of _____

Expenses	Budget	Actual
Subtotals		

Income

Other Income

Total Income

Total Actual Expenses

Remaining Balance

Notes

Credits

Savings

Goals

Monthly Planner and Expense Tracker

Month of _____

Expenses	Budget	Actual
Subtotals		

Income
_____

Other Income
_____

Total Income
_____

Total Actual Expenses
_____

Remaining Balance
_____

Notes

Credits	Savings	Goals

Monthly Planner and Expense Tracker

Month of _____

Expenses	Budget	Actual
Subtotals		

Income
_____

Other Income
_____

Total Income
_____

Total Actual Expenses
_____

Remaining Balance
_____

Notes

Credits	Savings	Goals

Monthly Planner and Expense Tracker

Month of _____

Expenses	Budget	Actual
Subtotals		

Income
_____

Other Income
_____

Total Income
_____

Total Actual Expenses
_____

Remaining Balance
_____

Notes

Credits

Savings

Goals

Monthly Planner and Expense Tracker

Month of _____

Expenses	Budget	Actual
Subtotals		

Income _____

Other Income _____

Total Income _____

Total Actual Expenses _____

Remaining Balance _____

Notes

Credits	Savings	Goals

Monthly Planner and Expense Tracker

Month of _____

Expenses	Budget	Actual
Subtotals		

Income
_____

Other Income
_____

Total Income
_____

Total Actual Expenses
_____

Remaining Balance
_____

Notes

Credits	Savings	Goals

Monthly Planner and Expense Tracker

Month of _____

Expenses	Budget	Actual
Subtotals		

Income

Other Income

Total Income

Total Actual Expenses

Remaining Balance

Notes

Credits

Savings

Goals

Monthly Planner and Expense Tracker

Month of _____

Expenses	Budget	Actual
Subtotals		

Income
_____

Other Income
_____

Total Income
_____

Total Actual Expenses
_____

Remaining Balance
_____

Notes

Credits	Savings	Goals

Monthly Planner and Expense Tracker

Month of _____

Expenses	Budget	Actual
Subtotals		

Income

Other Income

Total Income

Total Actual Expenses

Remaining Balance

Notes

Credits

Savings

Goals

Monthly Planner and Expense Tracker

Month of _____

Expenses	Budget	Actual
Subtotals		

Income

Other Income

Total Income

Total Actual Expenses

Remaining Balance

Notes

Credits	Savings	Goals

Monthly Planner and Expense Tracker

Month of _____

Expenses	Budget	Actual
Subtotals		

Income
_____

Other Income
_____

Total Income
_____

Total Actual Expenses
_____

Remaining Balance
_____

Notes

Credits

Savings

Goals

Monthly Planner and Expense Tracker

Month of _____

Expenses	Budget	Actual
Subtotals		

Income

Other Income

Total Income

Total Actual Expenses

Remaining Balance

Notes

Credits

Savings

Goals

Monthly Planner and Expense Tracker

Month of _____

Expenses	Budget	Actual
Subtotals		

Income _____

Other Income _____

Total Income _____

Total Actual Expenses _____

Remaining Balance _____

Notes

Credits	Savings	Goals

Monthly Planner and Expense Tracker

Month of _____

Expenses	Budget	Actual
Subtotals		

Income
_____

Other Income
_____

Total Income
_____

Total Actual Expenses
_____

Remaining Balance
_____

Notes

Credits	Savings	Goals

Monthly Planner and Expense Tracker

Month of _____

Expenses	Budget	Actual
Subtotals		

Income _____

Other Income _____

Total Income _____

Total Actual Expenses _____

Remaining Balance _____

Notes

Credits	Savings	Goals

Monthly Planner and Expense Tracker

Month of _____

Expenses	Budget	Actual
Subtotals		

Income
_____

Other Income
_____

Total Income
_____

Total Actual Expenses
_____

Remaining Balance
_____

Notes

Credits	Savings	Goals

Monthly Planner and Expense Tracker

Month of _____

Expenses	Budget	Actual
Subtotals		

Income
_____

Other Income
_____

Total Income
_____

Total Actual Expenses
_____

Remaining Balance
_____

Notes

Credits	Savings	Goals

Monthly Planner and Expense Tracker

Month of _____

Expenses	Budget	Actual
Subtotals		

Income
_____

Other Income
_____

Total Income
_____

Total Actual Expenses
_____

Remaining Balance
_____

Notes

Credits

Savings

Goals

Monthly Planner and Expense Tracker

Month of _____

Expenses	Budget	Actual
Subtotals		

Income _____

Other Income _____

Total Income _____

Total Actual Expenses _____

Remaining Balance _____

Notes

Credits

Savings

Goals

Monthly Planner and Expense Tracker

Month of _____

Expenses	Budget	Actual
Subtotals		

Income
_____

Other Income
_____

Total Income
_____

Total Actual Expenses
_____

Remaining Balance
_____

Notes

Credits	Savings	Goals

Monthly Planner and Expense Tracker

Month of _____

Expenses	Budget	Actual
Subtotals		

Income

Other Income

Total Income

Total Actual Expenses

Remaining Balance

Notes

Credits

Savings

Goals

Monthly Planner and Expense Tracker

Month of _____

Expenses	Budget	Actual
Subtotals		

Income
_____

Other Income
_____

Total Income
_____

Total Actual Expenses
_____

Remaining Balance
_____

Notes

Credits	Savings	Goals

Monthly Planner and Expense Tracker

Month of _____

Expenses	Budget	Actual
Subtotals		

Income _____

Other Income _____

Total Income _____

Total Actual Expenses _____

Remaining Balance _____

Notes

Credits	Savings	Goals

Monthly Planner and Expense Tracker

Month of _____

Expenses	Budget	Actual
Subtotals		

Income
_____
Other Income
_____
Total Income
_____
Total Actual Expenses
_____
Remaining Balance
_____
Notes

Credits

Savings

Goals

Monthly Planner and Expense Tracker

Month of _____

Expenses	Budget	Actual
Subtotals		

Income _____

Other Income _____

Total Income _____

Total Actual Expenses _____

Remaining Balance _____

Notes

Credits	Savings	Goals

Monthly Planner and Expense Tracker

Month of _____

Expenses	Budget	Actual
Subtotals		

Income _____

Other Income _____

Total Income _____

Total Actual Expenses _____

Remaining Balance _____

Notes

Credits	Savings	Goals

Monthly Planner and Expense Tracker

Month of _____

Expenses	Budget	Actual
Subtotals		

Income

Other Income

Total Income

Total Actual Expenses

Remaining Balance

Notes

Credits	Savings	Goals

Monthly Planner and Expense Tracker

Month of _____

Expenses	Budget	Actual
Subtotals		

Income
_____

Other Income
_____

Total Income
_____

Total Actual Expenses
_____

Remaining Balance
_____

Notes

Credits	Savings	Goals

Monthly Planner and Expense Tracker

Month of _____

Expenses	Budget	Actual
Subtotals		

Income _____

Other Income _____

Total Income _____

Total Actual Expenses _____

Remaining Balance _____

Notes

Credits	Savings	Goals

Monthly Planner and Expense Tracker

Month of _____

Expenses	Budget	Actual
Subtotals		

Income
_____
Other Income
_____
Total Income
_____
Total Actual Expenses
_____
Remaining Balance
_____
Notes

Credits	Savings	Goals

Monthly Planner and Expense Tracker

Month of _____

Expenses	Budget	Actual
Subtotals		

Income
_____

Other Income
_____

Total Income
_____

Total Actual Expenses
_____

Remaining Balance
_____

Notes

Credits	Savings	Goals

Monthly Planner and Expense Tracker

Month of _____

Expenses	Budget	Actual
Subtotals		

Income
_____

Other Income
_____

Total Income
_____

Total Actual Expenses
_____

Remaining Balance
_____

Notes

Credits	Savings	Goals

Monthly Planner and Expense Tracker

Month of _____

Expenses	Budget	Actual
Subtotals		

Income _____

Other Income _____

Total Income _____

Total Actual Expenses _____

Remaining Balance _____

Notes

Credits	Savings	Goals

Monthly Planner and Expense Tracker

Month of _____

Expenses	Budget	Actual
Subtotals		

Income _____

Other Income _____

Total Income _____

Total Actual Expenses _____

Remaining Balance _____

Notes

Credits

Savings

Goals

Monthly Planner and Expense Tracker

Month of _____

Expenses	Budget	Actual
Subtotals		

Income

Other Income

Total Income

Total Actual Expenses

Remaining Balance

Notes

Credits	Savings	Goals

Monthly Planner and Expense Tracker

Month of _____

Expenses	Budget	Actual
Subtotals		

Income _____

Other Income _____

Total Income _____

Total Actual Expenses _____

Remaining Balance _____

Notes

Credits	Savings	Goals

Monthly Planner and Expense Tracker

Month of _____

Expenses	Budget	Actual
Subtotals		

Income
_____

Other Income
_____

Total Income
_____

Total Actual Expenses
_____

Remaining Balance
_____

Notes

Credits

Savings

Goals

Monthly Planner and Expense Tracker

Month of _____

Expenses	Budget	Actual
Subtotals		

Income
_____

Other Income
_____

Total Income
_____

Total Actual Expenses
_____

Remaining Balance
_____

Notes

Credits	Savings	Goals

www.ingramcontent.com/pod-product-compliance
Lightning Source LLC
Chambersburg PA
CBHW081438220526
45466CB00008B/2434